ONE NATION FOR ALL
IMMIGRANTS IN THE UNITED STATES

# LIFE AS A SYRIAN AMERICAN

ELLEN CREAGER

PowerKiDS press

Published in 2018 by The Rosen Publishing Group, Inc.
29 East 21st Street, New York, NY 10010

Cataloging-in-Publication Data

Names: Creager, Ellen.

Title: Life as a Syrian American / Ellen Creager.

Description: New York : PowerKids Press, 2018. | Series: One nation for all: immigrants in the United States | Includes index.

Identifiers: LCCN ISBN 9781538323441 (pbk.) | ISBN 9781538322482 (library bound) | ISBN 9781538323458 (6 pack)

Subjects: LCSH: Refugees--Syria--Juvenile literature. | Immigrants--United States--Juvenile literature.

Classification: LCC HV640.5.S97 C74 2018 | DDC 362.7'7914095691--dc23



Developed and produced for Rosen by BlueApple*Works* Inc.
Art Director: T.J. Choleva
Managing Editor for BlueApple*Works*: Melissa McClellan
Designer: Joshua Avramson
Photo Research: Jane Reid
Editor: Marcia Abramson

Photo Credits: Cover clockwise: Les Cunliffe/Dreamstime.com; Isaiahlove/Dreamstime.com; thomas koch/Shutterstock.com Jazzmany/Shutterstock.com title page IM_photo/Shutterstock.com; flag Les Cunliffe/Dreamstime; background HorenkO/Shutterstock; p. 4 Jazzmany/Shutterstock.com; p. 6 Nice_Media/Shutterstock.com; p. 7 UTBP/Shutterstock; p. 8 Serban Bogdan/Shutterstock; p. 11 thomas koch/Shutterstock.com; p. 14 Public Domain; p. 16 Jim West/Alamy Stock Photo; p. 19 Tolga Sezgin/Shutterstock.com; p. 20 ZUMA Press, Inc./Alamy Stock Photo; p. 22 DFID - UK Department for International Development/Creative Commons; p. 24 Jim Grover/Alamy Stock Photo; p. 26 Matthew Yohe/Creative Commons; p. 28 WENN Ltd/Alamy Stock Photo



Manufactured in the United States of America

CPSIA Compliance Information: Batch BW18PK: For Further Information contact Rosen Publishing, New York, New York at 1-800-237-9932.

# CONTENTS

U.S. citizens with roots in the country of Syria are known as Syrian Americans.

# WHO ARE SYRIAN AMERICANS?

Syrian Americans have been part of the United States since the late 1800s. Hardworking and ambitious, the early settlers found success in their new country as merchants and business people. Part of the nation's **melting pot** of cultures, Syrian Americans have achieved their piece of the American Dream. Today, more than 170,000 Americans can trace their heritage to Syria.

Now there is a new chapter. Starting in 2015, a new wave of Syrians began to arrive on American soil. Unlike earlier immigrants, they were **refugees**, unable to go home even if they wanted to. Fleeing **civil war** in Syria, they sought a safe place to live.

Syrian immigrant parents work hard to provide for their families and help their children become successful.

They want a chance to work and do well. They want their children to be happy. They want to be safe. They want a new home.

They have come to America to find it.

"At first, I was really depressed," said a Syrian American woman who recently moved from Syria to Michigan. "I could not work. I had to keep asking people to speak more slowly because my English wasn't good. I couldn't get an apartment because I had no credit and no one to co-sign the papers. But now, I have a car, I have a home, and I'm happy."

... DID YOU KNOW? ...

## The Statue of Liberty

"Give me your tired, your poor, your huddled masses yearning to breathe free."

Those are the words on the base of the Statue of Liberty. They have inspired immigrants for more than 130 years.

The statue stands on tiny Liberty Island in the middle of New York Harbor in New York City. She was a gift from the people of France in 1889. Made of copper, with an iron frame interior, she was designed by French sculptor Frederic Bartholdi. Her interior frame was designed by Gustave Eiffel – yes, the same man who would go on to design the Eiffel Tower in Paris.

In the early 1900s, most immigrants to America arrived on boats. The boats sailed right past the Statue of Liberty. Immigrants' hearts lifted when they saw the grand statue that seemed to be inviting them into the United States.

Today, most immigrants fly to their destinations, so they do not see Lady Liberty when they arrive. Still, she is so famous that she remains an **emblem** of freedom for the world.

In 2016, about 17 million people lived in Syria, down from 22 million in 2012.

# HISTORY OF SYRIA

Because of recent civil war, Syria is at a crossroads in its history. Humans have lived there for at least 100,000 years. Great civilizations have risen and fallen. Caravans of traders have traveled its winding roads since ancient times.

Modern-day Syria is in the Middle East. To the north is the country of Turkey. To the east is the country of Iraq. To the west are the Mediterranean Sea and the country of Lebanon. To the south and southwest are the countries of Jordan and Israel.

Syria is green and fertile in the northwest and on its Mediterranean coast. The rest of the land is dry. Before the war, many tourists came to see the country's cultural sights and natural beauty.

About the same size as the U.S. state of Washington, Syria covers 71,000 square miles (114,263 sq km) and has 14 provinces. Its largest cities are Aleppo and the capital of Damascus. Both cities are among the oldest in the world, because people have lived there for 2,500 to 5,000 years.

Syria's official language is Arabic, and most Syrians are Arabs, although there are people of other ethnicities including Kurds and Americans. About 87 percent of Syrians are of the **Muslim** religion (mostly of the Sunni sect), while 10 percent are Christian and 3 percent are **Druze**.

## ANCIENT SYRIA

Thousands of years ago, many empires, groups, and tribes wrangled to control what is now Syria. Groups that came and went included the Amorites, Egyptians, Babylonians, Aramaeans, Persians, and Assyrians (which historians believe is the source of the name "Syria"). Then came the Greeks, Romans, Arabs, Turks, Mamluks from Egypt, and Christian Crusaders from Europe.

In 1516 "Greater Syria," as it was called, became part of the **Ottoman Empire** of Turkey. In 1918, just after World War I, Greater Syria was broken into four parts: Syria, Lebanon, Jordan, and Palestine, with the European nations of Britain and France splitting up their rule. France was in charge of Syria. For nearly 30 years, Syrian children even learned French in schools.

Syrian refugees, camped near Turkey, joined a wave of protests in June 2011.

Some Syrians, especially Jews and Christians, wanted no part of all the changes. Many emigrated to North America, South America, or Europe.

In 1946, Syria finally became independent. However, the nation continued to face challenges. Hafez al-Assad became president in 1971. The **dictator** brought stability, but he was a harsh ruler for 29 years. After he died in 2000, his son Bashar al-Assad became president.

He also ruled harshly. By 2011, Syria's people began protesting for changes and more freedom. President al-Assad refused to leave. That led to civil war. Rebels fought government forces all across the country.

Hundreds of thousands of Syrian refugees have crossed to Greek islands in small boats.

## THE TERRIBLE WAR

Years of war brought death and destruction. Between 2011 and 2017, an estimated 400,000 people died in the Syrian fighting, including both soldiers and citizens. By 2016, more than 13 million Syrians desperately needed help. About 6.3 million of them had no home.

In addition, by 2017, five million Syrians had fled to refugee camps in nearby Egypt, Iraq, Jordan, Lebanon, and Turkey. Some Syrians tried to get even farther away, applying to immigrate to places like the United States. Others boarded dangerous, overcrowded boats to cross the Mediterranean Sea to Europe.

During the war, Syria's economy had collapsed by half. There was no peace. The president even used chemical weapons to kill his own citizens. Even worse, a **terrorist** group called ISIS took over parts of Syria, causing terror.

... DID YOU KNOW? ...

### A Plague of ISIS

ISIS is a group that was founded in 2014. It is made up of radical terrorists from many nations who want an extreme form of Islam to take over the world. Muslims around the world have criticized ISIS as a fanatic **fringe group** that does not represent their religion.

ISIS took advantage of Syria's wartime **chaos**. They took control of towns and villages that could not fight back. They also occupied parts of the nearby country of Iraq.

Cruel and vicious, ISIS fighters executed people, murdered women and children, and wrecked cities and historic sites. They claimed to be religious but actually were criminals – stealing, killing, and hurting people.

As of 2017, ISIS controlled parts of Syria and neighboring Iraq. Many countries were fighting hard to destroy the group.

Many early Syrian immigrants started out in New York City. Some became peddlers like this food vendor in Manhattan.

# COMING TO AMERICA

In the late 1800s and early 1900s, Syrian Christian and Jewish families began arriving in the United States. Things were unstable in Syria, so they sought a new life in America, making their way mostly as merchants and grocers, peddlers, and textile sellers, and dreaming that their children would be safe and successful.

Between 1899 and 1932 more than 106,000 people came from Greater Syria to the U.S. (the actual country of Syria was not independent yet). Among the first to arrive were the Arbeelys from Damascus. They came in 1878 with eight family members, settling in New York, then Tennessee.

Other Syrian families followed. Many changed their names to sound more American. They learned English and became an integral part of American culture.

As many as 10,000 Syrian Americans are doctors. About 42 percent have professional or managerial jobs.

Jewish families settled mostly in New York and New Jersey. Christian families settled in Michigan to work in Detroit's auto industry, or in California and other states.

Immigration slowed between 1924 and 1965 because of strict U.S. laws. Even after laws changed, immigrant numbers from Syria were small. By 1970, only 15,000 people born in Syria lived in the United States. By 2015, the total was 83,000. That may sound like a lot, but it wasn't. Syrian natives totaled less than one half of 1 percent of the foreign-born population of the United States.

Up until 2015, in fact, Syrian immigrants to the U.S. numbered only a few thousand per year. They came for education, jobs, or to join family members. The war in Syria changed that.

In 2015, there were many Syrians in refugee camps who needed to immigrate to a new country. The United States, which had admitted only 36 Syrians as refugees in 2013, allowed 1,682 of refugees in 2015 and 12,587 in 2016.

## STATISTICS

Syrian Americans who immigrated before 2015 typically made a good median household income of $52,000 per year (with half of families earning more and half earning less). They were much more likely than the average American to hold a college degree and own a business. They mostly lived in Los Angeles, New York, Chicago, Detroit, or Pennsylvania.

Syrians who immigrated starting in 2015 were nearly all refugees. Half of the refugees were children under age 14. There were also many women. Most were not coming to the United States straight from Syria, but from refugee camps in Jordan and Turkey, where some had been living for five years or more.

About 98 percent of Syrian refugees were Muslims. Many had mental or physical health problems due to wartime **trauma** or injuries.

Social services groups helped refugees settle around the nation, with most of them in California, Michigan, Texas, and Arizona. Thirty-one states announced they did not want Syrian refugees. These states claimed they were afraid that terrorists posing as refugees might slip into the country, even though no Syrian American had ever harmed the United States.

Agencies sent the refugees to cities that welcomed them warmly. Many Syrian refugees have done amazing things in their new communities. In Phoenix, Arizona, organizations helped Syrian refugees hold a bake sale, selling delicious Syrian pastries. The money went to refugee families. In Detroit, many Syrian refugees have volunteered by feeding people in need.

Then in early 2017, the new U.S. president, Donald Trump, ordered that no more Syrian refugees would be allowed in the country.

Many Syrians formed schools in refugee camps because education is very important to Syrians.

A federal court judge blocked the order. Still, the door began closing to Syrian refugees.

In the first three months of his presidency, Trump's administration allowed just 1,221 Syrian refugees to come into the United States. Others would have to wait.

Some Syrian American women choose to wear headscarves.

# LIVING AS AMERICANS

Syrian Americans find different ways of celebrating their own culture and taking part in American culture. Some may feel pressure to assimilate to American culture.

One Syrian American (whose mother and grandparents immigrated to Michigan from Homs, Syria, in 1929) said her childhood goal was to try to be as "American" as possible.

"We lived in a community where everybody had blond hair and blue eyes, and we had olive skin and dark eyes," she remembered. "My mother made Syrian dishes, and I ate them, but I didn't want to. I wanted to be completely American."

She and her brothers and sisters all grew up highly educated. Now, they live in cities across the country. One of her sisters still makes traditional Syrian food at the holidays.

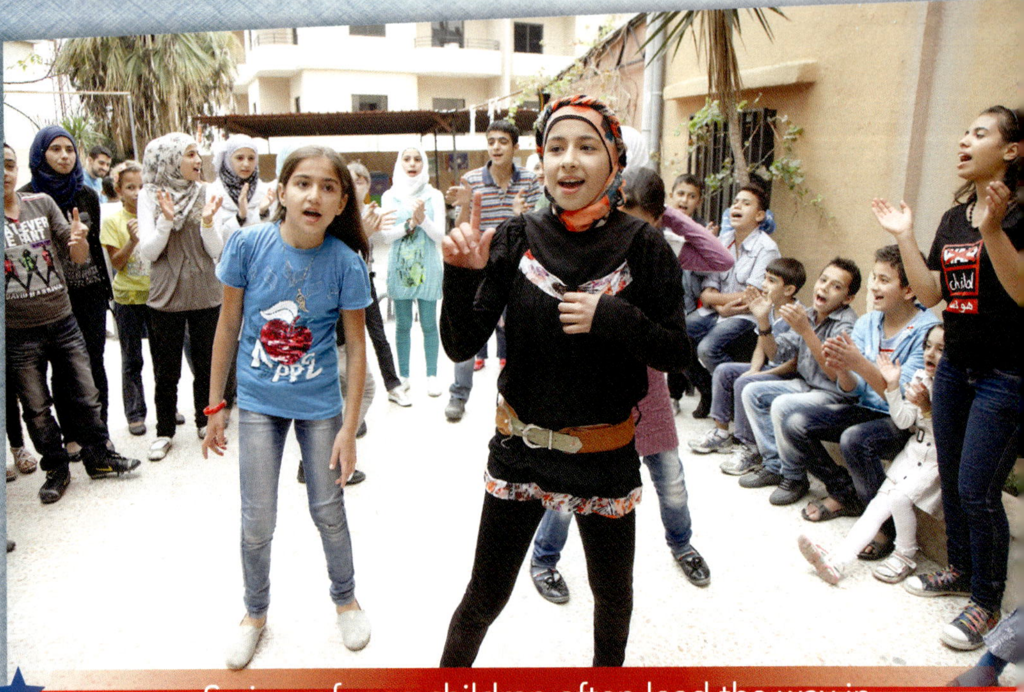

Syrian refugee children often lead the way in helping their families adjust to a new home.

Some Syrian Americans still live in close-knit communities and continue to practice Syrian customs. The Lehigh Valley region near Allentown, Pennsylvania, for example, has about 5,200 residents of Syrian descent.

Syrian Americans can also find support through their common places of worship. Syrian Christians may find friendship in their churches, which are mostly **Eastern Orthodox**. Syrian Jews may find comfort through their synagogues and temples. Syrian Muslims may find the same peace at their local mosques.

## NEWEST SYRIAN AMERICANS

Recent refugees are just beginning their journey as Americans. If they are lucky, they are placed near resources that cater to Arab Americans. Being near Arab grocery stores, bakeries, butchers, community centers, and social services helps them adjust to their new life in America.

"In Syria, we walk a lot. We walk to the grocery store to get fruit and vegetables and meat, or we take small buses. New refugees often ask to live near a grocery store or near another Syrian family or a school," said a Syrian American caseworker in Michigan who helps new refugees. Because she is a recent immigrant herself, she understands the refugees' worries.

"Syrians are really social people and don't like to live alone. We like to live near common areas," she said, adding that being a new refugee is a confusing experience at first.

"When a family first arrives, they are in shock, really, and really depressed. Everything is new. But after five or six months, you see them and they are changed. They are happy. They like the safety and freedom here. I see how changed they are, and how proud they are of themselves," she said.

New refugees are given 90 days' worth of help including food programs, health insurance, and job counseling. If the adults in the family are disabled or can't find work, they may face financial struggles when this support ends. If they can work, their future is more secure. Nationwide, associations such as the Multifaith Alliance for Syrian Refugees and Syrian American Medical Society work for Syrians both in the United States and in the refugee camps.

As families adjust to their new home, they may find that food, holidays, and other traditions are ways that Syrian Americans can hold on to their heritage.

Syrians who lived in a city in their home country and received an education may have an easier time adapting to the United States than those who lived in the Syrian countryside.

... DID YOU KNOW? ...

### Delicious Syrian Food

Syrian American food combines the best of Middle East traditions. Among the popular dishes:

**Manoushi:** Puffy Syrian flatbread

**Shorbit Adas:** Lentil soup

**Tabouli:** Salad made of **bulgur** wheat, parsley, and tomato

**Beewaz:** Parsley salad

**Sayadieh:** Rice and onions with fresh fish

**Dawood Basha:** Syrian meatballs

★ **Traditions:** In Syria, a baby's first tooth is cause for a big celebration. They serve a dessert, sliha, made of wheat berries, pomegranate seeds, nuts, and coconut.

★ **Holidays:** Syrian Christians celebrate Christmas and Easter. Jews celebrate special holidays like the Jewish New Year and Yom Kippur. Muslims practice a period of fasting called Ramadan and the celebration afterward, Eid al-Fitr.

★ **Dress:** Syrian Americans tend to dress like other Americans. Muslim Syrian American women may wear headscarves called hijab to cover their hair.

Steve Jobs led the creation of the iPhone, iPod, and other famous products at Apple.

# AMAZING ACHIEVEMENTS

Many Syrian Americans have contributed incredible things to their new home and the world. Here are some famous Syrian Americans:

★ **Steve Jobs:** Co-founder of possibly the most famous company in the world, Apple Computer (now Apple, Inc.). Born in 1955, he died in 2011. Jobs was adopted, but his biological father was an immigrant from Homs, Syria.

★ **Paula Abdul:** The singing star and choreographer was born in 1962 in California. Her father is from Aleppo, Syria.

★ **Mitch Daniels:** Former governor of Indiana; president of Purdue University. Born in 1949 in Pennsylvania. His grandparents were from Syria.

★ **Brandon Saad:** Hockey player for the Pittsburgh Penguins. Born 1992 in Pennsylvania. His father is from Syria.

★ **Paul Anka:** Pop singer. Born in Ottawa, Canada in 1941, he became a U.S. citizen in 1990. His father was from Syria.

★ **Jerry Seinfeld:** The comedian and producer was born in 1954 in Brooklyn, N.Y. His mother's family were Jewish immigrants from Aleppo, Syria.

★ **F. Murray Abraham:** Academy Award-winning actor who played the composer Mozart in the film *Amadeus*. He was born in Pennsylvania in 1939. His father was from Syria.

★ **Isaac Mizrahi:** Fashion designer. He was born in New York in 1961. His parents are from Syria.

Comedian Jerry Seinfeld received an Ellis Island Family Heritage Award in 2009. One set of his grandparents came to New York from Syria.

... **DID YOU KNOW?** ...

### He invented the ice cream cone

Ernest Hamwi, a Syrian American vendor at the 1904 St. Louis World's Fair, was selling a Syrian waffle pastry called zalabia. The vendor next to him was selling ice cream.

One day, Hamwi rolled his waffle into a **cornucopia** cone shape. The ice cream man started selling the cones filled with ice cream, and soon, everyone wanted the cornucopia dessert.

Hamwi went on to found the Cornucopia Waffle Company and other ice cream cone factories.

Born in Damascus, Syria, he died in the United States in 1943 a wealthy man. His invention brought happiness to millions.

Although some other people claim to have thought up the idea of the ice cream cone first, Hamwi is given credit for its birth in American culture. It's a sweet story of success.

★ Yasser Seirawan: Chess grandmaster and four-time U.S. chess champion. Born in Damascus, Syria, in 1960, he immigrated to the United States when he was seven years old.

What will the next generation of Syrian Americans achieve in the future? Just wait and see.

# Glossary

**bulgur** Cracked wheat, used in cooking.

**chaos** Total confusion and disorder.

**civil war** Two or more groups in the same country fighting each other.

**cornucopia** A receptacle shaped like a horn or cone.

**dictator** A leader who can't be voted out.

**Druze** A small religious group that originated in Islam.

**Eastern Orthodox** Christian churches that started in the eastern Roman Empire.

**emblem** An object or figure that suggests an idea.

**fringe group** People who share extreme or unusual ideas.

**melting pot** Blending of cultures, races, and groups into one.

**Muslim** A person who follows the religion of Islam and the teachings of Muhammad.

**Ottoman Empire** Area ruled by Turkey from the thirteenth to twentieth century.

**refugee** A person who flees home or country to go somewhere safer.

**terrorist** A person who uses violence against innocent people to try to achieve a goal.

**trauma** Extreme distress.

# For More Information

## Further Reading

Capek, Michael. *Understanding Syria Today.*
Newark, DE: Mitchell Lane Publishers, 2014.

Mason, Helen. *A Refugee's Journey from Syria.*
New York: Crabtree Publishing Company, 2017.

South, Coleman. *Syria.*
New York: Cavendish Square Publishing, 2016.

Yomtov, Nel. *Syria.*
New York: Scholastic, 2013.

## Websites

Due to the changing nature of Internet links, PowerKids Press has developed an online list of websites related to the subject of this book. This site is updated regularly. Please use this link to access the list:
**www.powerkidslinks.com/cs/syrianam**

# Index